micro**Quests**

amazing DNA

Rebecca L. Johnson

illustrations by Jack Desrocher

diagrams by Jennifer E. Fairman, CMI

M Millbrook Press • Minneapolis

for Eric—RLJ

Many of the photographs in this book are micrographs. Micrographs are photos taken through a microscope. Sometimes bright colors are added to micrographs to make cell parts easier to see. Other times, cells are stained with dye so cells and cell structures show up more clearly under a microscope.

As you read this book, look for the bold words in colored boxes. These words tell you about the photos and diagrams. You can also look for the lines that connect the photos and the text.

Text copyright © 2008 by Rebecca L. Johnson
Diagrams on pp. 5, 9, 12–13, 14, 15, 16–17, 19, 22, 24, 34, 37, 38, 40 copyright © 2008 by Fairman Studios, LLC
Other illustrations copyright © 2008 by Lerner Publishing Group, Inc.

Millbrook Press, Inc.
A division of Lerner Publishing Group, Inc.
241 First Avenue North
Minneapolis, MN 55401 U.S.A.

Website address: www.lernerbooks.com

Library of Congress Cataloging-in-Publication Data

Johnson, Rebecca L.
  Amazing DNA / by Rebecca L. Johnson ; illustrations by Jack Desrocher ; diagrams by Jennifer E. Fairman.
       p. cm. — (Microquests)
  Includes index.
  ISBN 978-0-8225-7139-1 (lib. bdg. : alk. paper)
  1. DNA—Juvenile literature. I. Desrocher, Jack, ill. II. Title.
QP624.J64 2008
  572.8'6—dc22

Manufactured in the United States of America
1 2 3 4 5 6 – DP – 13 12 11 10 09 08

table of contents

1. **DNA is everywhere** 4

2. **building bodies** 8

3. **making copies** 12

4. **from plans to proteins** . 18

5. **how genes build us** 26

6. **mistakes, bad and good** . 37

glossary 44

read more about DNA 46

index 47

chapter 1

DNA is everywhere

Brown eyes. A turned-up nose. A dimple that gets deeper when you smile. It's your face. You know it well. And unless you have an identical twin, you know that nobody else looks just like you.

What forms your features? They're made up of cells. Cells are the smallest units of life. They are the building blocks of living things. Everything from mushrooms and mice to plants and people is built of cells.

A single cell is very small. You have billions of cells in your arm. You have about 100 trillion cells in your whole body.

Not all your cells are the same. They come in different shapes and sizes. They do different things. But all the cells in your body have one thing in common. You must look deep inside a cell to find it.

If you look at a cell under a microscope, you'll see a dark, rounded shape in the middle. That's the cell's nucleus. The nucleus is sometimes called the control center of the cell. We're looking for something inside the nucleus.
There—see those thin strands?
Those strands are DNA.

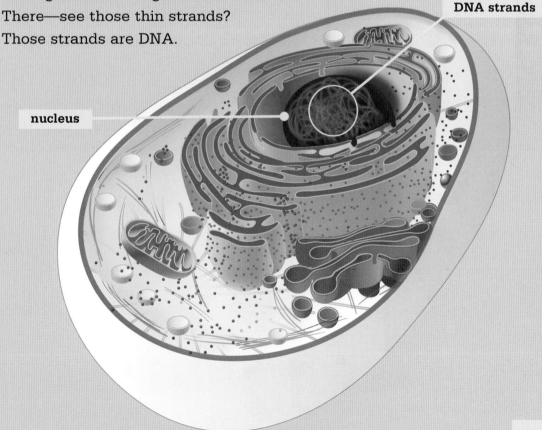

DNA strands

nucleus

What about the **nerve cells** in your brain? Each one has DNA strands in its nucleus. And a **skin cell** on your toe? DNA strands are in its nucleus too. Every nucleus in every cell in your body is packed with DNA strands. So what are they?

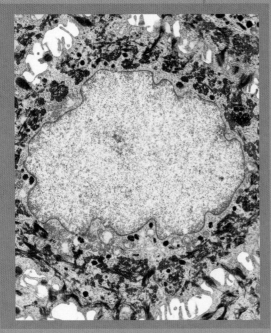

The letters DNA stand for deoxyribonucleic acid. By itself, DNA is not a living thing. It's a molecule. Molecules are groups of atoms. Atoms are extremely small particles. They are too small to see with a microscope. Atoms make up everything in the universe.

DNA is a very long molecule. Stretched out, the DNA from just one of your cells is about 10 feet (3 meters) long. And if you stretched out the DNA from all your cells? That would reach from Earth to Pluto and back—twenty times!

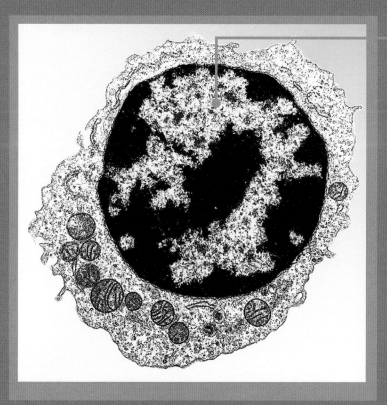

Strands of DNA look like hardly anything at all. Yet they are probably the most important structures in your body. They are more important than your skin, muscles, or bones. They are even more important than your heart or brain.

building bodies

DNA is the key to building cells. Without DNA, you wouldn't have cells. Without cells, you wouldn't have anything that cells make. You wouldn't have a heart, lungs, or brain. Without DNA, you wouldn't exist.

DNA is like a set of building plans. It has all the information needed to build a complete living thing. Your DNA contains the plan for building you.

DNA is also in charge of keeping your body alive. DNA is the master molecule. It holds the secret of life.

SECRET OF LIFE

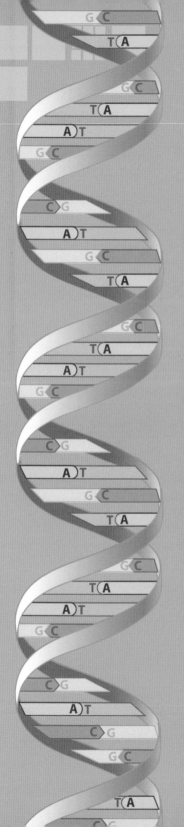

To understand how DNA can do so many things, you have to understand its shape. Under a microscope, DNA may look like a single thread. But it's actually made of two long strands. Short pieces connect the strands.

The long strands and the short pieces form a sort of ladder. The long strands are the sides of the ladder. The connecting pieces are the ladder's rungs. But while a regular ladder is straight, DNA is twisted.

Each rung of the DNA ladder is formed from two parts. Scientists call these parts bases. DNA has four bases. They are adenine, thymine, guanine, and cytosine. To make things simpler, they have nicknames. Adenine is A, thymine is T, guanine is G, and cytosine is C.

DNA carries information in its bases. The way the bases are arranged is the key to how DNA can copy itself. DNA copies itself so that the information it carries can be passed on to other cells.

Long ago, inside your mother's body, you began life as one cell. That **first cell** divided to become many.

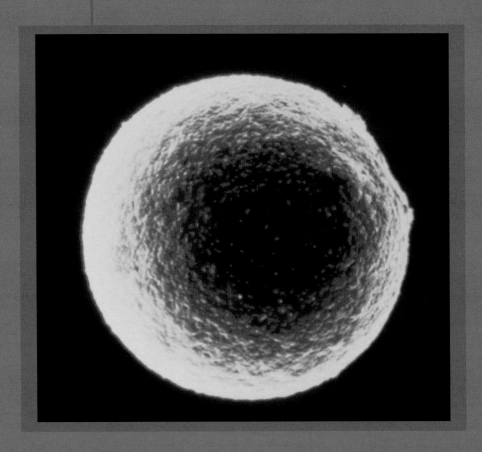

During millions and millions of cell divisions, the DNA in your first cell was copied again and again. Each new cell received the same DNA. It got the same set of plans for building your body as all the other cells.

Think about the different kinds of cells that make up your body. They all contain exactly the same DNA. Since you're built from trillions of cells, that means trillions of DNA copies.

chapter 3

making copies

How does DNA copying work? First, DNA splits down the middle. Then it makes two identical molecules where before there was one.

DNA copying sounds complicated. But it makes sense if you take it step-by-step.

First, imagine untwisting a strand of DNA. Take a close look at the bases (the rungs of the ladder). You already know that each rung is formed from two bases. The two bases are linked, or bonded, together. Two linked bases form a base pair.

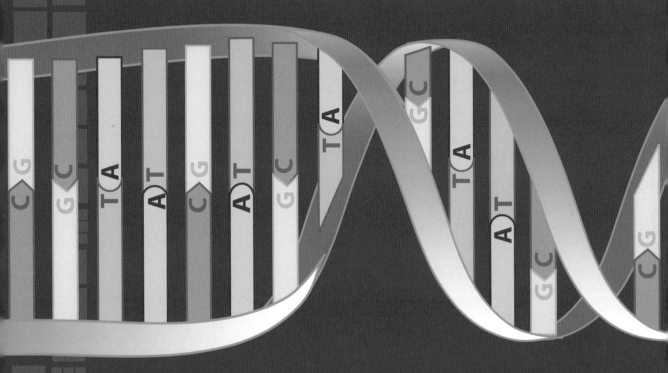

Not all bases can bond together. Base C always links to base G (and G to C). A always bonds to T (and T to A). The bases in every DNA molecule bond in this way.

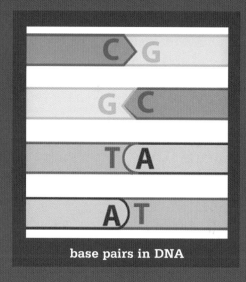

base pairs in DNA

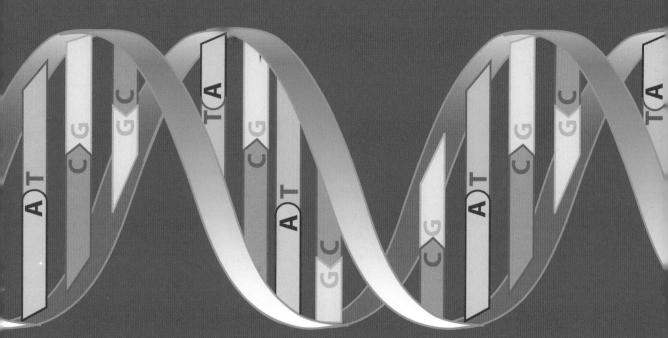

Base pairs can unlink too. When DNA unwinds, base pairs begin to separate, one after another. It's like a zipper being unzipped.

The **DNA double strand splits into two single strands.** On each strand, unlinked bases—half rungs of the ladder—are exposed. The exposed bases on the separated strands form a template. A template is a pattern for making copies of something.

Each strand of DNA is a template on which a new strand can be built. That new strand will be exactly like the one that was there before.

To copy DNA, a cell needs extra DNA bases. A cell's nucleus has lots of free DNA bases inside it.

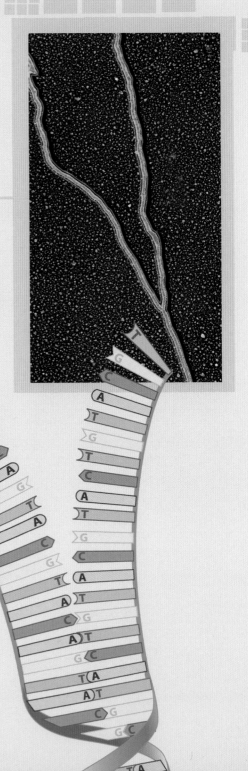

Here's how it works. The DNA molecule has unzipped. The two strands are separated. The bases on each of the unzipped strands are exposed. Some of the free bases move toward them. A's bond to T's. T's bond to A's. C's bond to G's. And G's bond to C's. One after another, the new bases settle into place.

free bases

Each original strand now has a new strand next to it. Each new strand is exactly like the strand it replaced. That's true down to every A, T, C, and G.

One DNA molecule has become two. The two new molecules are identical copies of the original one. And they are identical to each other. Once the copying is done, the two DNA molecules twist back up into spiral shapes.

original DNA strand

new DNA strand

DNA copying is called DNA replication. It usually takes place just before cells divide. Cells divide to make new cells. Living things need new cells so they can grow. New cells also replace those that wear out and die. As you read this, millions of cell divisions are taking place in your body. Cells are dividing in your skin. They're dividing in your stomach and intestines. They're even dividing inside your bones!

When a cell divides, the two new cells each get their own copy of the original cell's DNA. The two cells have identical DNA. That DNA is also identical to the DNA in the original cell.

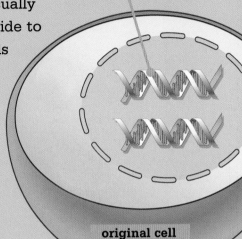

replicated DNA, greatly enlarged

original cell

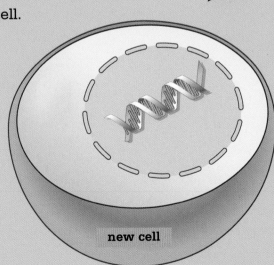

new cell

Thanks to DNA copying, each one of your body cells ends up with the same DNA. Every cell has an identical set of body-building plans.

Fine, you may be thinking. Every cell has a set of plans. But how are those plans used? How do tiny, twisted strands of DNA build a whole person?

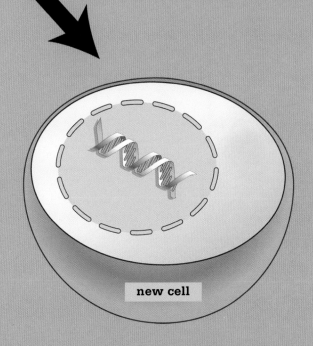

new cell

from plans to proteins

Have you ever made cookies or a cake? Then you've followed a recipe. DNA is pretty much a set of recipes. DNA recipes are for making chemicals called proteins.

Proteins are molecules. They are the building blocks of cells. Proteins also carry out special jobs. Some proteins do their jobs inside the cell that makes them. Others work in various parts of the body.

The DNA inside your cells holds the recipes to make about fifty thousand different proteins. That's more than enough to build a body like yours.

DNA's protein recipes are written in a code. The code uses the A's, T's, C's, and G's in DNA base pairs.

These four bases are like letters in words. Together they spell out messages. Those messages are instructions for building proteins. The order of the bases tells what proteins need to be built. A-T-C-C-T-G-A-A-G might spell out part of the code for one protein. C-T-T-A-A-A-G-C-G-T-A-T might spell out part of the code for another.

Four letters may not seem like enough to code for thousands of different proteins. But think of how much information a computer can hold. Computer code is written with only two numbers (just 0's and 1's). The DNA code has four letters (or bases). It can hold much more information than a computer.

The long sections of DNA bases that code for proteins are called genes. Each gene codes for a different protein.

Here's an example. Hemoglobin is a substance found in your red blood cells. Its job is to carry a gas called oxygen. Every cell in your body needs oxygen to live. You breathe in oxygen from the air. That oxygen moves from your lungs into your blood. It is picked up by hemoglobin and carried to cells.

Hemoglobin is made from two proteins. Scientists have named one of these proteins HBB. The gene that codes for HBB is 1,600 bases long. The code starts out like this:

tggctgaggcaggagaattgcttgaacccagg
aggcagaggttgcggtgagcctagattgcacc
attgcactctagcttgggcaatagggatgaaac
tccatctcagaagagaaaagaaaaaaagacctt
attctgttatacaaatcctctcaatgcaatccatat
agaataaacatgtaaccagatctcccaatgtgta
aaatcatttcaggtagaacagaattaaagtgaa
aagccaagtctttggaattaacagacaaagatc
aaataacagtcctcatggccttagaatttacct
aacattttttttagaatcaattttcttatatatgaat
tggaaacataatcctccctcacaaacacattcta

HBB is just one of the thousands of proteins your body needs. The genes in your DNA code for all of them. Human DNA has about 20,000 to 25,000 different genes. Some proteins are built with the help of more than one gene.

Together, all your genes form your genetic code. That's the complete set of chemical instructions needed to build your body and keep it running. Your genetic code is unique to you. No one else (unless you have an identical twin) has exactly the same set of genes that you have.

So genes are a set of coded instructions. But how are those instructions turned into proteins? In other words, how do the recipes get made?

Let's say a cell needs to make HBB. In the cell's nucleus, the section of DNA that contains the HBB gene unwinds. Then the strands unzip.

Next, extra bases pair up with the exposed bases on the unzipped strands. But in this case RNA, not DNA, bases are used. RNA stands for ribonucleic acid. RNA is similar to DNA. Three of its bases are the same (A, C, and G). But instead of thymine (T), RNA contains uracil (U). Like T, however, U always pairs with A.

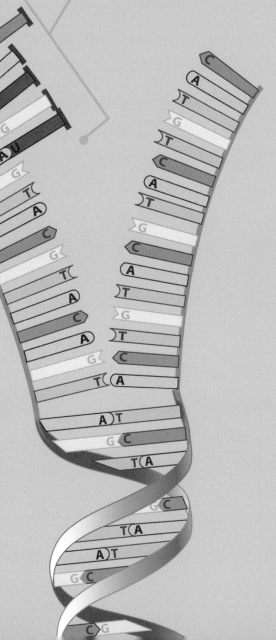

newly forming RNA strand

One by one, RNA bases move into place. They bond to the exposed bases along the DNA strand. They also bond to one another. They form a growing strand of RNA.

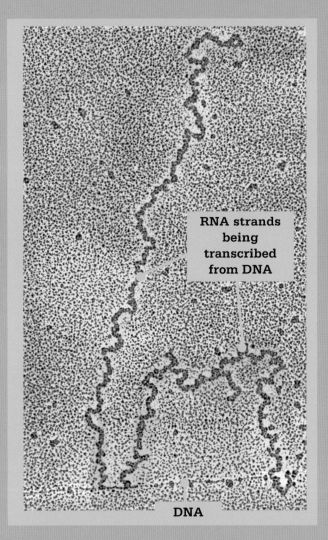

RNA strands being transcribed from DNA

DNA

Finally, the last base is added. The single strand of RNA pulls free. The double-stranded DNA molecule zips up and twists together again. The RNA strand is a copy of the information on the HBB gene. It's the full set of instructions for making HBB.

This copying process is called transcription. That's because information from DNA is rewritten or transcribed into RNA. The RNA copy is called messenger RNA (mRNA for short). It is now ready to do its job.

Like a real messenger, mRNA carries information from one place to another. It leaves the nucleus and heads for a ribosome out in the cell. Ribosomes are small, rounded structures. They build proteins.

The mRNA attaches to a ribosome. The ribosome begins reading the mRNA's code. Think of the code as being made up of words. Together, those words form a sentence. The sentence describes HBB.

Each word tells the ribosome to grab a certain amino acid. Amino acids are small molecules that join together to make proteins. Your body has twenty different kinds of amino acids. By joining in different ways, these twenty amino acids can make thousands of different proteins. A cell contains lots of free amino acids. They are ready and waiting to be used.

protein

messenger RNA

amino acids

ribosome

The ribosome "reads" each word of the code on the mRNA strand. Then it adds the correct amino acid to the chain of amino acids that form the protein. Making a protein from an mRNA strand is called translation. That's a pretty good name for the process. The language of genes (a series of bases) is translated into the language of proteins (a series of amino acids).

Word by word, the ribosome reads the gene sentence. Amino acid by amino acid, it builds the protein. It's finished when the final amino acid slips into place.

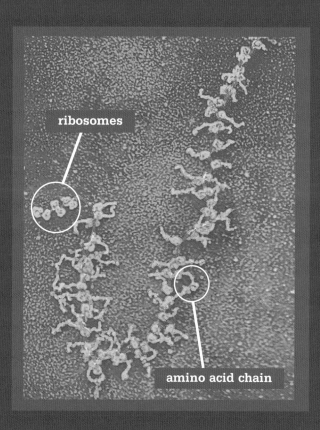

ribosomes

amino acid chain

The chain of amino acids is now a protein. As soon as it's done, the protein twists and folds. Its shape is just the right shape for the protein to do its job.

how genes build us

Every minute, millions of proteins are being made in every cell in your body. But not all your cells are making the same kinds of proteins.

In different cells, mRNA is transcribing different genes. So different cells are making different proteins.

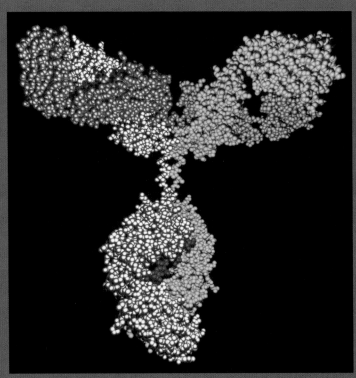

computer-generated image of a protein

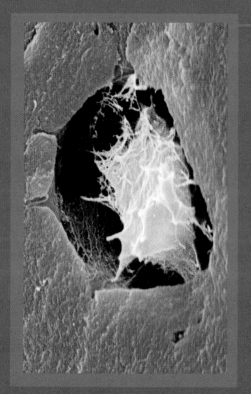

Take a **bone cell** and a **white blood cell**. Both cells have exactly the same DNA. But certain genes are being transcribed in the bone cell. Other genes are being transcribed in the white blood cell. These cells have different jobs. They need to make different proteins.

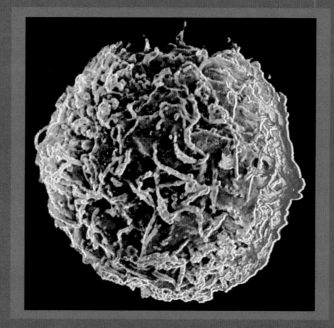

Your genes play a big role in how you look. They control the color of your eyes. They determine the shape of your nose and toes. These are physical traits. Traits are the result of genes at work. They reflect the information stored in your DNA.

Earth is home to millions of living things. They range from toadstools to trees and hummingbirds to whales. All of them have DNA. Like your DNA, theirs has A's, T's, C's, and G's. Their A's bond to T's. Their C's link to G's. Just like yours.

If all living things have DNA, why is a beetle so different from a bear? Why is a cockroach not like a cockatoo? The answer has to with the order of all of those A's, T's, C's, and G's along strands of DNA. If you put letters in a different order, you get different words. If you put bases in a different order, you get different genes.

And what does having different genes mean? It means different proteins, cells, and entire organisms.

Even so, you're not as different from other organisms as you might think. You may not look much like a fruit fly. But you share 36 percent of your genes with one. You share 85 percent with a zebra fish. You have 98 percent of your genes in common with a chimpanzee.

You have even more in common with the genes of other people. But for many years, scientists didn't know how many genes people had. In the 1990s, scientists set out to discover the exact sequence of all the bases in human DNA. By doing this, they hoped to identify all the genes in the human genome. Genome is another name for all the genetic information carried by a living thing.

Scientists completed the Human Genome Project in 2003. They discovered that human DNA is made from about 2.9 billion bases. These bases form between 20,000 and 25,000 genes.

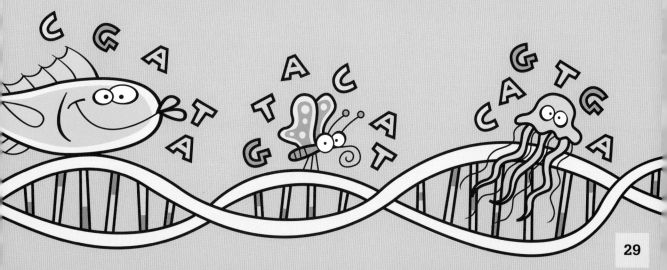

Genetically, you're related to every other person on the planet. In fact, 99.5 percent of your genes are just like everybody else's. But your DNA most closely matches that of your **family members**.

People with closely matched DNA often share many traits. Maybe you have dimples like your mother. Or a chin like your father. The passing on of traits from parents to their children is called heredity.

How do traits get passed? To understand this, you need to know a bit more about DNA.

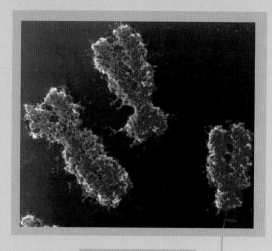

Most of the time, DNA looks like a lot of tangled strands inside the nucleus. Just before a cell divides, though, the strands begin to scrunch up. The scrunched-up strands form clumps. These clumps are called **chromosomes**.

If you lined up all the chromosomes from one of the cells of a girl's body, they would look like this. Notice that the chromosomes form **twenty-three pairs**. That means there are forty-six chromosomes in all. The two chromosomes in each pair are very similar. Pair number twenty-two is the exception. That's the pair that makes you a boy or a girl. A girl's twenty-second pair is a matched set. It has two X chromosomes. But a boy's twenty-second pair includes one X and one smaller Y chromosome.

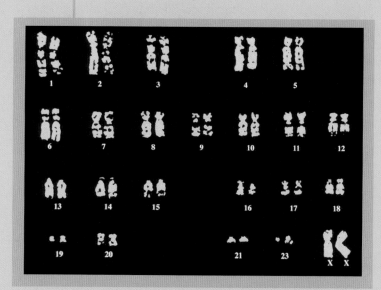

Twenty-three of your chromosomes (one member of each chromosome pair) are from your mother. They were in an **egg cell** made in her body. The other twenty-three chromosomes came from your father. They were in a **sperm cell** made in his body.

When the sperm cell and the egg cell joined, they formed a fertilized egg. That was your very first cell. It had a total of forty-six chromosomes, organized into twenty-three pairs.

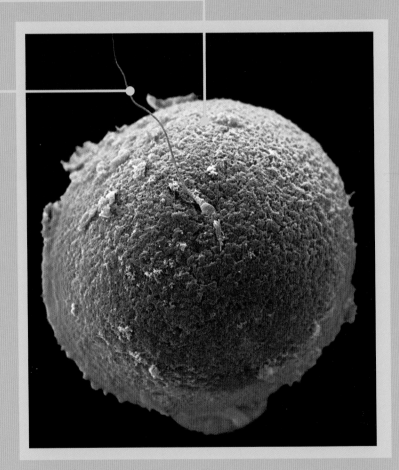

Each member of a chromosome pair contains similar genes. The genes are located at similar points on the two chromosomes. These matching genes carry instructions for producing particular traits. (They do this by coding for specific proteins, as you already know.)

But matched genes on a pair of chromosomes are not usually identical. For any given pair of genes, the gene that came from your mother is probably slightly different from the gene that came from your father. Different forms of the same gene are called **alleles**.

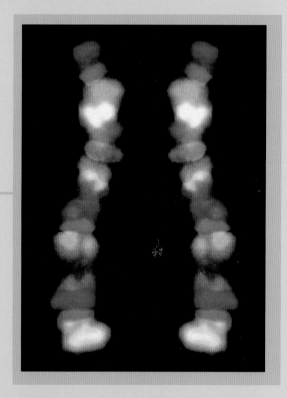

Alleles of a particular gene both code for the same trait. But since they are not identical, tiny differences, or variations, are possible. These little variations mean that many traits you inherit from your parents are similar to theirs. But they're not exactly the same.

Some of your traits may not resemble those of your parents at all. Such traits could be the result of new combinations of alleles. These new combinations are created when eggs and sperm are formed. During the process, alleles on pairs of chromosomes swap places. This is called crossing over. Crossing over produces new combinations of alleles on chromosomes. You inherited new combinations of alleles from your parents. That's why you have some traits that are unique to you.

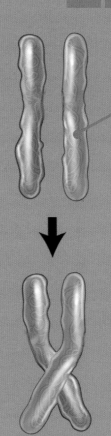

chromosome

Some traits are controlled by only two forms (alleles) of a single gene. The **shape of your hairline** is a good example. One allele for the trait says, "Put a peak in the hairline." The other says, "No peak in the hairline." What your hairline looks like depends on which "hairline" alleles you inherited.

Most traits are trickier. They are controlled by more than one gene. Traits like **eye color** and hair color are determined by several genes. Other traits are the work of many genes. Figuring out how lots of genes interact to produce a trait is not easy.

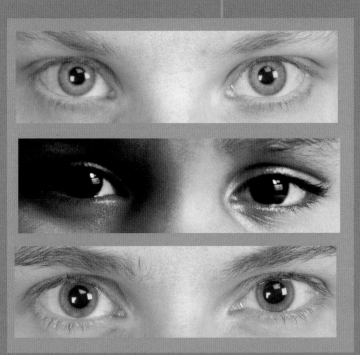

In terms of traits, genes are important. But they aren't everything.

Perhaps you were born with fair skin. Your genes are responsible for that. But spend a few days in the summer sun. Your skin will darken. Or perhaps your genes programmed your body to grow tall. A poor diet could limit how tall you'll be.

Remember that genes code for proteins. Proteins are the raw materials of traits. The final form that those raw materials take depends on what happens in and around you. Genes and your surroundings together make you what you are.

mistakes, bad and good

Something else also influences traits: gene mutations. A mutation is a change in a gene.

Some mutations happen when DNA is being copied before a cell divides. Outside factors cause other mutations. Certain kinds of rays in sunlight can cause mutations. So can X-rays and some chemicals. Sometimes, mutations just happen for no reason at all.

A small mutation along a stretch of DNA can make a big difference. Say a sequence of bases, T-A-C, mutates into T-G-C. The change is like a misspelled word. When mRNA copies the gene with that misspelled word, the mistake will be copied too.

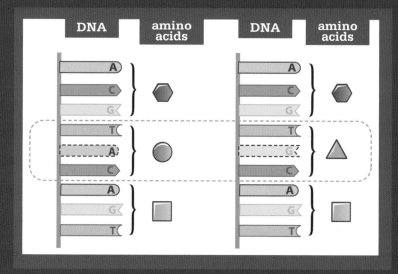

The T-G-C sequence could code for the wrong amino acid. When a protein is made, it will contain a mistake. The protein might not work the way it's supposed to.

Imagine what would happen if a mutation added an extra base to a gene. That extra letter would change the code from that point on. It would change the words in the gene's protein recipe. In this example, you can see how adding an extra G changes which amino acids the gene codes for.

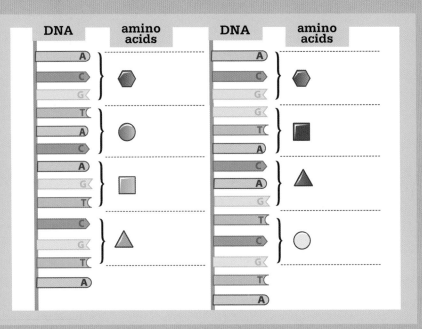

Changing the words in the recipe might mean the wrong amino acids would be made. The wrong amino acids would form the wrong protein. That wrong protein might mess up other proteins. The cell might have a hard time doing its job. It might even die.

Mutations can also cause a cell to start dividing when it shouldn't. Cell division gone wild can lead to a disease called cancer. Some types of cancer are serious threats to health.

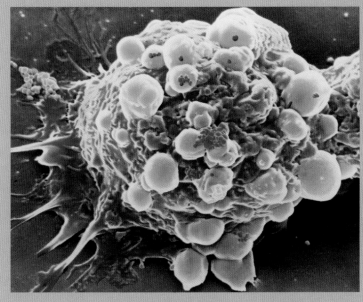

cancer cell

Here's a bit of good news. Small mistakes in DNA can often be fixed. Your cells have special proteins that check DNA strands. They look for small mistakes in the genetic code. If they find a mistake, they can often correct it.

Even if the mistake can't be fixed, all is not lost. A mutation in one cell might mean death for that cell. But you have trillions of cells. Losing a few to mutations isn't a problem. Your body replaces damaged and dying cells all the time by normal cell division.

But DNA mutations in egg and sperm cells can have a more lasting effect. When eggs and sperm with mutations come together, they create fertilized eggs that have those mutations too.

A mutation might kill a fertilized egg cell. But suppose it doesn't. When the egg cell divides, its DNA will be copied. The copies will go to the two new cells that are produced. The same will be true when those cells divide. Eventually, there will be millions of cells. All will have DNA identical to the first cell. All will carry the mutation that the first cell had.

Imagine that the organism formed from those millions of cells is a penguin. A mutation causes black spots on its chest. The penguin goes on to reproduce. The mutation it carries will be passed on to its young, or offspring. Then the offspring reproduce. The mutation will live on, passed from one generation to the next.

Some inherited mutations are harmful. They can cause problems for living things. Sickle-cell anemia is an inherited mutation in people. A small change in the DNA causes red blood cells to be long and curved instead of round. These **"sickled" cells** have trouble moving in the blood. Sickle-cell anemia can make people very sick. It can even cause death.

Other inherited mutations aren't as bad. Take color blindness. It's caused by a mutation on the X-chromosome. People who are color blind cannot tell the difference between certain colors. Being color blind affects how you see the world. But it won't kill you.

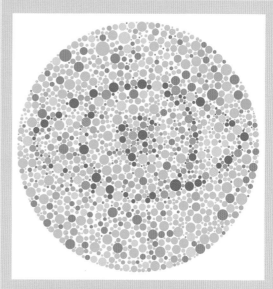

People with one form of color blindness cannot see the red shape in the green circle.

41

Some mutations don't seem to make any difference at all. But one day, one of these mutations might turn out to be good. Why? Mutations are the source of genetic variation. Genetic variation means new combinations of genes. The world around us changes all the time. To survive, living things must adjust, or adapt, to these changes.

Adapting is possible thanks to genetic variations. How? Imagine there is a group of creatures called zorks. Every zork has the same basic DNA. But each one has slightly different combinations of alleles for their traits.

Suppose the zorks' world warms up. Most zorks can't stand the heat. As the temperature climbs, they get sick and die. A few zorks don't die. Because of a genetic variation, they can stand the heat. A small difference in their DNA helps them survive.

SURVI

The survivors reproduce. They pass on the helpful genetic variation to their offspring. Their offspring also survive the heat. Like their parents, they can live in a warmer world.

That's how small differences in DNA can make a big difference in life. Genetic variations help living things change over time.

DNA builds cells and bodies. Your DNA has shaped you since the moment you came into being. Remember that the next time you look in a mirror. That face looking back at you? **It's really a reflection of your DNA, the amazing molecule hard at work deep in your cells.**

glossary

adapt: to change in a way that helps survival

alleles: slightly different forms of the same gene

amino acid: a small molecule that is a building block of proteins

atoms: extremely small particles that make up everything in the universe

base pair: one "rung" on DNA's ladder-like molecule. It consists of two bases bonded together.

base: the variable part of a DNA (or RNA) molecule. DNA contains the four bases adenine, thymine, cytosine, and guanine. RNA contains adenine, cytosine, guanine, and uracil.

cells: the smallest units of life. Cells are the building blocks of living things.

chromosomes: clumps of DNA that in a cell's nucleus. Chromosomes contain genes.

crossing over: the exchange of genetic material by similar chromosomes

DNA (deoxyribonucleic acid): a very long molecule that stores coded information for building living things

gene: a sequence of DNA bases that codes for a specific protein. Genes are responsible for hereditary traits.

genetic code: the coded information about building and operating an organism carried in that organism's DNA

genome: an organism's total amount of genetic information

heredity: the passing on of traits from parent organisms to their offspring

inherited: passed from parents to offspring

mRNA (messenger RNA): a strand of RNA that carries coded information from DNA to ribosomes

molecule: a group of atoms

mutation: a change in DNA

nucleus: a rounded structure that is a cell's control center

offspring: new living things made by reproducing. Children are offspring of human parents.

proteins: molecules that are the building blocks of cells

replication: the process of copying a DNA molecule

ribosome: a tiny, rounded structure inside cells that puts together amino acids to make proteins

RNA (ribonucleic acid): a molecule that carries information coded in genes. RNA is similar to DNA but has the base uracil instead of thymine.

template: a pattern for making copies of something

traits: characteristics of a living thing that are coded for in its DNA

transcription: the process of copying information from DNA to mRNA

translation: the process of using information carried by mRNA to make a protein

variation: a slight difference

read more about DNA

Books

Fridell, Ron. *Genetic Engineering.* Minneapolis: Lerner Publications Company, 2006.

Phelan, Glen. *Double Helix: The Quest to Uncover the Structure of DNA.* Washington, DC: National Geographic, 2006.

Walker, Richard, and Steve Jones. *Genes and DNA.* London: Kingfisher, 2003.

Websites

DNA (PBS)
http://www.pbs.org/wnet/dna/
This PBS website discusses the history of the discovery of DNA with photographs, diagrams, and videos.

DNA from the Beginning (Dolan DNA Learning Center)
http:www.dnaftb.org/
This site contains an extensive study of genetics featuring explanations, videos, biographies, and links to other websites.

DNA Interactive (Cold Spring Harbor Laboratory)
http://www.dnai.org/
At this site, learning about DNA is presented in a series of problems to be solved through investigations featuring photos, diagrams, and videos.

Gene Gateway: Exploring Genes and Genetic Disorders (Human Genome Project)
http:www.ornl.gov/sci/techresources/Human_Genome/posters/chromosome/hbb.shtml
This websites describes the gene that causes sickle-cell anemia and shows the structures of the proteins involved.

Learn Genetics. (University of Utah Genetic Science Learning Center)
http://learn.genetics.utah.edu/units/basics/tour
This tour of genetics gives simple explanations of DNA with interesting graphics.

index

adenine (A), 9, 13, 15, 19, 22, 28, 37
alleles, 33–35
amino acids, 24–25, 37–38
anemia, 41
atoms, 6

base, 9–10, 12–15, 19–20, 22–23, 25, 28–29, 37–38
base pair, 12, 14
blood, 20, 41
bones, 7, 16
bone cell, 27
brain, 7–8

cancer, 39
cell division, 11, 16, 39, 40
chromosomes, 31–34, 41
crossing over, 34
cytosine (C), 9, 13, 15, 19, 22, 28, 37

DNA copying, 10–11, 12, 14–17, 37, 40

egg cell, 10, 32, 40

genetic code, 21, 39
genetic variation, 42–43
genes, 20–23, 25–30, 33–38, 42
genome, 29
guanine (G), 9, 13, 15, 19, 22, 28, 37

HBB, 20–24
heart, 7–8
hemoglobin, 20
heredity, 30
Human Genome Project, 29

intestines, 16

lungs, 8, 20

messenger RNA (mRNA), 23–26, 37
muscles, 7
mutation, 37–42

nerve cells, 6
nucleus, 5–6, 14, 22, 24, 31

organism, 28–29, 40
oxygen, 20

protein, 18–22, 24–28, 33, 36–38

red blood cells, 20, 41
ribonucleic acid (RNA), 22–23
ribosomes, 24–25

skin, 7, 16, 36
skin cells, 6
sperm, 40
sperm cell, 32, 40
stomach, 16

thymine (T), 9, 13, 15, 19, 22, 28, 37
traits, 27, 30, 33–37
transcription, 22–23, 26–27
translation, 24–25

uracil (U), 22

white blood cells, 27

about the author

Rebecca L. Johnson is the author of many award-winning science books for children. Her previous books include the Biomes of North America series, *The Digestive System, The Muscular System, Genetics,* and *Plate Tectonics.* Ms. Johnson lives in Sioux Falls, South Dakota.

photo acknowledgments

Photographs in this book are used with the permission of: © Michael Abbey/Photo Researchers, Inc., p. 6 (top); © Steve Gschmeissner /Photo Researchers, Inc., p. 6 (bottom); © Dr. Gopal Murti/Visuals Unlimited, pp. 7, 14; © John Giannicchi/Photo Researchers, Inc., p. 10; © Dr Elena Kiseleva/Photo Researchers, Inc., pp. 23, 25; © Alfred Pasieka/Photo Researchers, Inc., p. 26; © SPL/Photo Researchers, Inc., p. 27 (left); © CNRI/Photo Researchers, Inc., p. 27 (right); © Stockbyte, pp. 30, 35 left (middle); © Eye of Science/Photo Researchers, Inc., pp. 31 (top), 32; © Biophoto Associates/Photo Researchers, Inc., p. 31 (bottom); © REGENTS OF UNIV. OF CALIFORNIA 2005/DR. ULI WEIER/Photo Researchers, Inc., p. 33; © age fotostock/SuperStock, p. 35 (right); © Sam Lund/Independent Picture Service, p. 35 left (top and bottom); © Quest/Photo Researchers, Inc., p. 39; © Omikron/Photo Researchers, Inc., p. 41 (top); © David Nicholls/Photo Researchers, Inc., p. 41 (bottom).

Front cover: © Dr. Gopal Murti/Visuals Unlimited (background), © Lerner Publishing Group, Inc. (illustration)